Exclusively

TRIVIA

by Anthony S. Pitch

Mino Publications
Potomac, Md.

Published by

Mino Publications
9009 Paddock Lane
Potomac, Md. 20854

Library of Congress Catalog Card No.
84-62046

ISBN 0-931719-00-3

Printed in the United States of America

To the memory of my brother, Leonard,
who was so gallant, so warm-hearted, so young

Also by Anthony S. Pitch

Exclusively Presidential Trivia
Exclusively First Ladies Trivia
Washington, D.C. Sightseers' Guide
Bazak Guide to Israel
Bazak Guide to Italy
Peace
Inside Zambia—And Out

Exclusively Washington Trivia is available at special bulk purchase discounts for sales promotions, conventions, fund raisers or premiums.

For details, write to

Mino Publications
9009 Paddock Lane
Potomac, Maryland 20854

1. Who was the model for the statue of a soldier on the facade of the American Legion building at 1608 K. St. N.W.?

2. How many females were among D.C.'s total population of 638,333 in the 1980 census?

3. Which Washingtonian is buried in a mausoleum with a stained glass window made by Tiffany of New York?

4. How did officers address the Marquis Marie Jean Paul Roch Yves Gilbert Motier de Lafayette during the Revolutionary War?

5. This President referred to his wife as "the boss"

6. Which great medical scientist experimented with mosquitoes at his Georgetown home, 3021 Q. St.?

7. How many gallons of water fill the lagoon in the Grand Hyatt Hotel?

8. This famed Washington *Redskins* coach was the son of an immigrant Italian butcher

9. As First Lady she held Sunday evening hymn sessions attended by Cabinet officers and Congressmen

ANSWERS

1. Lt. Hulon Whittington, awarded the Medal of Honor in World War II

2. 342,916

3. Brewing magnate, Christian Heurich

4. They called him Gilbert

5. Harry Truman

6. Walter Reed

7. 27,000

8. Vince Lombardi

9. Lucy Hayes

QUESTIONS

10. Guess the waist measurement of the heaviest U.S. President

11. Who wrote that the King of Denmark was "a regal-looking man"?

12. At what age was George Washington initiated into Masonry?

13. Where did the name Foggy Bottom originate?

14. The grandfather of this President was slain by Indians

15. What was the purpose of the 23rd Amendment?

16. What happened to the 31-ton pair of limestone eagles sculptured for the old Social Security building?

17. Why did the Washington *Senators* forfeit their final game at RFK Stadium?

18. What was the price of a Famous Milk Shake at Washington's 15 Hot Shoppes in 1955?

19. This late Supreme Court Associate Justice was once a member of the Ku Klux Klan

ANSWERS

10. 54"—William Howard Taft

11. Eisenhower's Chief of Protocol, Wiley Buchanan Jr.

12. 18

13. From the swirling haze over the former swamps stretching from the Potomac River to the Lincoln Memorial and H. St. N.W.

14. Abraham Lincoln

15. It enabled D.C. residents to vote in Presidential elections

16. They were chiseled into oblivion by the Arlington man who won them at an auction, because his wife objected to their size and the publicity

17. The fans tore up the turf and bases for souvenirs before the game was over

18. A quarter

19. Hugo Black

20. What happened to the man who shot President McKinley to death?

21. How was Harriet Beecher Stowe's *Uncle Tom's Cabin* published before it came out in book form?

22. Which plush hotel faces the AFL-CIO headquarters?

23. Broke at 21 and on his honeymoon, what job did Jack Kent Cooke have?

24. To whom did each of these Secret Service code names refer?
    a. Searchlight
    b. Deacon
    c. Passkey
    d. Woodcutter

25. What did Averell Harriman give his wife, Pamela, for a wedding present?

26. Where was Nancy Reagan lunching on the day her husband was shot?

27. Which modern convenience was installed in the National Theatre in the summer of 1946?

28. How many square miles make up the District of Columbia?

ANSWERS

20. Leon Czolgosz was electrocuted at Auburn, N.Y. in 1901

21. It was serialized in *The National Era*, a Washington newspaper

22. The Hay-Adams

23. Encyclopedia salesman

24. a. President Nixon
    b. President Carter
    c. President Ford
    d. Henry Kissinger

25. A portrait of Emma, Lady Hamilton, by George Romney

26. At Michael & Lucy Ainslie's Georgetown home

27. Air conditioning

28. 70

29. Where is the longest escalator outside of the Soviet Union?

30. Guess the age of the oldest person ever to sit in Congress

31. What was the star attraction at the auction sale of the *Washington Post* in 1933?

32. What job did Joe Gibbs have before joining the *Redskins?*

33. This First Lady spoke five languages

34. Why is there a statue of a 2-year-old girl on her rocking chair in Glenwood Cemetery?

35. In which government building is there a mural depicting the song recital of Marian Anderson at the Lincoln Memorial?

36. Why is the late Panchito still remembered for singing *Rock-a-by-baby* at the OAS Main Building?

37. How many U.S. Senators went on to become President?

38. During whose administration was the White House East Room used for bicycle races by the President's sons?

ANSWERS

29. At Metrorail's Bethesda stop (218 ft.)

30. Sen. Theodore Green (R.I.) was 93 when he retired in 1961

31. The Hope Diamond, worn by *Post* owner Mrs. Evalyn McLean

32. Offensive Coordinator of the San Diego *Chargers*

33. Lou Hoover

34. Her parents ordered it over her grave after she died of burns

35. Interior Department

36. He was a parrott

37. 15—most recently Richard Nixon

38. James Garfield

39. Taft Bridge, on Connecticut Avenue, was nicknamed something else for almost a quarter century

40. Why did *Redskins* teammates jocularly call Sonny Jurgensen "The Red Roach"?

41. What is the constant temperature of the giant panda's inside enclosure at the Zoo?

42. What is the link between the first U.S. bombing attack on North Vietnam and President Woodrow Wilson's car?

43. What was the name of the first store opened in Washington in 1880 by Mr. Woodward and Mr. Lothrop?

44. How tall was Abraham Lincoln?

45. Why did the Lord Chief Justice of England sit on the bench of the Supreme Court of the United States?

46. How many calls did the Fire Department respond to within 4 days of Martin Luther King's assassination?

47. Who was Jack Valenti's celebrity guest at the Academy Awards after Super Bowl XVII?

ANSWERS

39. "The Million Dollar Bridge"

40. Because he used to lift lunch bags from their lockers

41. 60 degrees fahrenheit

42. *Pierce Arrow* was the code-name for the air raid and also the make of the presidential auto

43. The Boston Dry Goods House

44. 6'4"

45. It was at the invitation of the U.S. Chief Justice, during a visit in 1883

46. 810

47. *Redskins* quarterback Joe Theismann

48. This First Lady's son wrote that "she has no appreciation for fine food"

49. This reopened landmark was the largest public/private restoration project in U.S. history

50. What is the average life of a dollar bill printed at the Bureau of Engraving & Printing?

51. Why did the Mayor of Tokyo have to send a second batch of gift cherry trees to Washington?

52. Where can you see a six-toed Native American?

53. Who was the first President to die in office?

54. Why did Congress, in 1839, ban duelling in the District of Columbia?

55. What is Admiral Farragut holding in his hands in his downtown statue?

56. Where did Mrs. Julia Ward Howe write *Battle Hymn of The Republic?*

57. What did Duke Ellington, born in D.C., call his first band?

ANSWERS

48. Eleanor Roosevelt

49. Union Station, costing about $160 million

50. 18 months

51. The first 2000 were infested with insect pests and plant diseases

52. In the painting, *Baptism of Pocahontas* in the Capitol's Rotunda

53. William Henry Harrison (1841)

54. A year earlier, Representative Jonathan Cilley of New Hampshire had died of gunshot wounds in a duel near Anacostia Bridge

55. A telescope

56. In Willard's Hotel

57. *The Washingtonians*

58. Which coach said "The opera isn't over until the fat lady sings"?

59. What was The Blue Jug?

60. What kind of airplane flew close to the Potomac River in 1896?

61. Who was the only President to serve two non-consecutive terms?

62. Who tied at 295 lbs. each as the heaviest *Redskins* of 1982?

63. Which former Congressional wife posed topless for *Playboy* magazine?

64. Which *Washington Post* columnist was a former book reviewer for the *Washington Star*?

65. What great institution is nicknamed "the nation's attic"?

66. When did Washington D.C. become the first major U.S. city to have a black majority?

67. Who was the news photographer whose picture formed the basis for the Iwo Jima memorial?

68. When did Metrorail open?

ANSWERS

58. The *Bullets'* Dick Motta

59. A 19th century D.C. jail, so-called because it was painted blue

60. A 25 lb. model, driven by steam

61. Grover Cleveland

62. Dave Butz and Joe Jacoby

63. Rita Jenrette

64. Mary McGrory

65. The Smithsonian

66. 1960

67. Joe Rosenthal

68. 1976

69. Who designed the Vietnam Veterans Memorial while a senior at Yale University?

70. What was the price tag for the new *Air Force One* Presidential Boeing 707 delivered in 1962?

71. Who was Howard University named after?

72. What sign greeted Queen Marie of Rumania as she was driven to Mt. Vernon during a State visit?

73. Who starred at Griffith Stadium in the first world heavyweight boxing championship fight in the Washington area?

74. What kind of pistol did John Wilkes Booth fire to kill Abraham Lincoln?

75. What privilege was stripped from the Dean of the Diplomatic Corps in 1981?

76. Which President never attended school and was taught to write by his wife?

77. Who was the star performer in the rebuilt Filene Center at Wolf Trap Farm Park?

ANSWERS

69. Maya Ying Lin

70. $7 million

71. Oliver Otis Howard

72. "Queen Marie—get your waffles here"

73. Joe Louis and Buddy Baer

74. A single-shot Deringer

75. The Soviet Ambassador was no longer allowed to park his limo in the State Department's underground garage

76. Andrew Johnson

77. Spanish tenor Placido Domingo

78. What did the National Symphony musicians use for a stage when they began summer concerts in 1936?

79. What treasure did Britain make available for display in the Capitol Rotunda during the U.S. Bicentennial?

80. Who won Washington's first professional major sports championship after 1942?

81. When did Congress agree to return to Virginia those lands originally ceded to form the District of Columbia?

82. How many acres does Union Station cover?

83. Where was composer John Philip Sousa born?

84. Why were the remains of Smithsonian founder, James Smithson, removed from an Italian cemetery and brought to the "castle" on the Mall?

85. Which Washington lawyer pressed General William Westmoreland's multi-million dollar libel suit against CBS?

86. Who was the bride at the first outdoor White House wedding?

ANSWERS

78. A barge, anchored on the Potomac River, beneath Memorial Bridge

79. An original copy of the Magna Carta, signed by King John in 1215

80. The *Bullets,* in capturing the NBA crown in 1978

81. 1846

82. 25

83. 636 G. St. S.E.

84. Genoese local authorities said the graves would have to be relocated because they needed the cemeterial land for quarrying

85. Dan Burt

86. Tricia Nixon

87. Where is the largest collection of Shakespeariana in the world?

88. What was President Ford's favorite radio show?

89. Who composed the song *Hail to the Redskins?*

90. What made Dr. Mary Walker the most eccentric woman in Washington?

91. How much did architect Benjamin Latrobe offer Italian sculptors and stone carvers to work on the Capitol?

92. Where did the leader of a Nazi sabotage team surrender to FBI agents in 1942?

93. How many of the 14.4 million people who visited Washington in 1983 stayed with friends or relatives?

94. Where will you find the largest collection of works by James McNeill Whistler in a single museum?

95. How many people visited the new Zoo on a single Sunday just over a century ago, when 73 animals were displayed?

ANSWERS

87. At the Folger Shakespeare Library

88. Harden & Weaver on WMAL

89. Barnee Breeskin

90. Awarded the Medal of Honor for her services as the only female surgeon in the Civil War, she dressed forever in men's clothing—with special sanction from Congress!

91. $3 a day plus all travel expenses

92. In room 351 of the Mayflower Hotel

93. 5.2 million

94. The Freer Gallery of Art

95. 30,000

QUESTIONS

96. Who was the first woman to see her son's Presidential inauguration?

97. Which world religious leader arrived in Washington by helicopter in 1979?

98. For whom did George Will work before becoming a columnist?

99. Why is the left ear missing from the marble head of Abraham Lincoln in the Capitol Rotunda?

100. Who was Sugar Ray Leonard named after?

101. How did James Forrestal die 2 months after resigning as Secretary of Defense?

102. How did former Attorney-General John Mitchell make history when he went to prison in the aftermath of Watergate?

103. In what year did the Washington *Senators* win the World Series?

104. What was Larry King's name before he went into radio broadcasting?

105. What is the largest manufacturing industry in the District of Columbia?

ANSWERS

96. Mrs. Eliza Garfield

97. Pope John Paul II

98. Senator Gordon Allott (R.-Colorado)

99. Sculptor Gutzon Borglum wanted to symbolize Lincoln's incomplete life

100. Blind singer/pianist Ray Charles

101. He leapt from a 13th floor window after suffering a nervous breakdown

102. He was the highest ranking government official ever sentenced to jail

103. 1924

104. Larry Zeiger

105. Printing and publishing

106. Who wrote *Conversations with Kennedy?*

107. What percentage of the sun's surface, viewed from Washington D.C., was eclipsed on May 30, 1984?

108. What well-known landmark was once called Pacific Circle?

109. Were buttons or zips sewn in the flies of President Reagan's size 42 suits?

110. Which First Lady said: "I am rather proud of the fact that after nearly a quarter of a century of marriage, my husband feels free to make his decisions and act on them without consulting me"

111. Who led the first exploration up the Potomac River by white sailors?

112. Which *Redskins'* quarterback was known as "Slinging Sammy"?

113. Whose graves are below the statue of *Grief* in Rock Creek Cemetery?

114. Why was Pearl Bailey dubbed "Washington's own Pearlie Mae"?

ANSWERS

106. Benjamin Bradlee

107. 94½ percent

108. Dupont Circle

109. Buttons

110. Grace Coolidge

111. Captain John Smith

112. Sam Baugh

113. Historian Henry Adams and his wife, Clover

114. Because of her frequent performances, particularly in the National Park Service's "Summer in the Parks" program

115. Which is the oldest law firm in the nation's capital?

116. Why did the Soviet Embassy dump the idea of buying the Virginian estate where Jacqueline Kennedy grew up?

117. What two suggested names were rejected in favor of The Chesapeake & Ohio Canal?

118. Where will you find the complete list of more than 3000 men and one woman who won the Congressional Medal of Honor?

119. How many record yards did John Riggins gain on an unprecedented 38 carries in Super Bowl XVII?

120. Where were diplomats of the Axis powers interned prior to their departure from the USA?

121. What landmark was raised 1/2000th of an inch during a seismic disturbance on August 31, 1886?

122. How many hundreds of thousands of people lived in Washington in 1950, during its peak population?

ANSWERS

115. Covington & Burling

116. They discovered that Virginia laws did not always recognize diplomatic immunity

117. Potomac Canal; Union Canal

118. In the Hall of Heroes at the Pentagon

119. 166

120. White Sulphur Springs, West Virginia

121. The Washington Monument

122. 800,000

123. How did a Paris art dealer tempt Washington's Mr. & Mrs. Duncan Phillips to buy Renoir's *Luncheon of the Boating Party?*

124. Why was President Ford told to drive around the block when he arrived for a reception at the British Embassy?

125. Which former British Chief of the Imperial General Staff is buried in Arlington National Cemetery?

126. Whom did Robert Shoffner succeed as Wining & Dining Editor of *The Washingtonian?*

127. Who arrived in Washington as a Senate page with $60 in his pocket and two decades later had an estimated $2 million?

128. What was the score at Super Bowl XVII?

129. When she won *Vogue's Prix de Paris* in 1951, Jacqueline Bouvier (later Kennedy) wrote that she wished she had known these three persons

130. Which bridge has a row of sculptured Indian heads made from a life mask of Chief Kicking Bear?

ANSWERS

123. He hung it in his apartment then invited them to dine there

124. He arrived earlier than his hostess, The Queen

125. Sir John Dill

126. Charles & Frances Turgeon

127. Wheeler-dealer Bobby Baker

128. *Redskins* 27 *Dolphins* 17

129. Oscar Wilde, Charles Baudelaire and Sergei Diaghilev

130. Dumbarton Bridge, also known as Buffalo Bridge, at Q. St. N.W.

131. Who remains the only woman to have had a husband and a son who were Presidents?

132. What is the average annual temperature in Washington?

133. Who was called "His Honesty, the President"?

134. Who was the first reigning European monarch to visit the United States?

135. What did Bob Hope have in common with Vice-President Spiro Agnew?

136. What was the connection between Peggy O'Neale, daughter of a 19th century Washington inn-keeper, and the French Rothschilds?

137. Who was the first President-elect to arrive in Washington by train?

138. Who was the first President to leave Washington by train at the end of his term?

139. Which church has a 1000 lb. bell made from a British cannon captured in the War of 1812?

ANSWERS

131. Abigail Adams

132. 57.3 degrees fahrenheit

133. Rutherford Hayes

134. King Albert of Belgium

135. Peter Malatesta, aide to Agnew, was Hope's nephew

136. Her granddaughter married a Rothschild

137. William Henry Harrison

138. Andrew Jackson

139. St. John's Church on Lafayette Square

QUESTIONS

140. When was the National Press Club founded?

141. Who decided to build the Capital Centre after the NHL awarded Washington a hockey franchise?

142. Where can you see and hear the news read in 40 languages?

143. Which Washington landmark is named after a poor Latvian immigrant who died a billionaire in 1981?

144. How did the FBI describe The Hopkins Institute it raided near Connecticut Ave./ Woodley Rd. N.W. in 1943?

145. Which Grande Dame referred to her mastectomies as ''going topless''

146. Guess the total acreage of the U.S. National Arboretum

147. What incident prompted creation of the Protocol Office in the State Department?

148. What is inaccurate about the painting *Declaration of Independence* in the Capitol Rotunda?

ANSWERS

140. 1908

141. Abe Pollin

142. The Voice of America studios

143. The Hirshhorn Museum & Sculpture Garden

144. "The most notorious call(girl) house in the East."

145. Alice Roosevelt Longworth

146. 444 acres

147. The annual diplomatic dinner at the White House in 1927, when the wife of the Belgian Ambassador refused to sit next to the German Ambassador

148. Five of the 47 people portrayed were not signatories to the Declaration of Independence, and 14 who did sign it do not appear

149. How was Orlando Letelier, former Chilean Ambassador to the USA, assassinated?

150. Guess how much the National Gallery of Art paid the ruler of Liechtenstein for Leonardo da Vinci's painting, *Ginevra de'Benci*

151. What was the annual operating cost of the Presidential yacht *Sequoia* before it was auctioned off in the Carter years?

152. Name the great leader of his time whose statue straddles the territory of two countries

153. During the hot season this President never slept at the White House, riding instead to the Soldiers' Home north of Washington

154. Which Chief Justice of the Supreme Court fell from a step-ladder in the law library and remarked: "That time I was completely floored"?

155. Since 1946 every Superintendent of the U.S. Naval Observatory has held this military rank

156. On what condition did a benefactor donate Mitchell Playground in Kalorama to the District of Columbia?

ANSWERS

149. His booby-trapped car exploded, in Sheridan Circle

150. A "fantastically high" price which the Gallery keeps secret in agreement with the royal vendor

151. Nearly $800,000

152. Sir Winston Churchill, whose statue stands in front of the British Embassy. One leg is in embassy property, the other outside

153. Abraham Lincoln

154. John Marshall

155. Captain

156. That the city government forever take care of the grave of her pet poodle

157. Which embassy owns the 40-room mansion built for Alvin Lothrop, founding partner of Woodward & Lothrop?

158. When did Sugar Ray Leonard win his Olympic boxing title?

159. Who was known as "The sage of Anacostia"?

160. Which Washington philanthropist wrote his grandchildren: "The most valuable bequest I can make you is a good name"?

161. This leading 19th century hotel was named after its black founder, a one-time cook in the American embassy in London

162. Who were the first five recipients of the annual Kennedy Center Honors?

163. On what Federal property can you find one of the finest arboretums in the world?

164. Why are a father and son remembered for two events relating to Ulysses J. Grant?

165. How long had the Washington *Senators* been in the capital before moving to Texas?

ANSWERS

157. The Soviet

158. 1976

159. Frederick Douglass

160. W. W. Corcoran

161. Wormley's

162. Marian Anderson, Fred Astaire, George
     Balanchine, Richard Rogers and Arthur
     Rubinstein

163. Capitol Hill

164. Dr. George Shrady, the father, attended
     Grant during his last illness. Henry Shrady,
     the son, sculptured the Grant Memorial at the
     east end of the Mall

165. 71 years

166. Why did Jane Pierce stay away from her husband's inauguration in 1853?

167. On what occasion did Union and Confederate veterans march together for the first time?

168. Who was the first President to be mourned with a funeral procession down Pennsylvania Avenue?

169. Which political spouse was nicknamed *Joan of Art* because of her encouragement of the arts?

170. When were the first degrees conferred by the American University?

171. Who was the male star in the movie *D. C. Cab*, filmed in Washington?

172. How tall was Lyndon Johnson?

173. What became known as the "David and Goliath diplomatic duel"?

174. Why did Margaret Truman exclaim that she couldn't go to the door to say goodbye to the Queen of England?

175. When did four B-29s make the first non-stop flight from Japan to National Airport?

ANSWERS

166. She was still mourning the death of her sole surviving son in a train derailment two months earlier

167. The World War I Victory Parade in 1919 down Pennsylvania Avenue

168. William Henry Harrison, who died in office in 1841

169. Joan Mondale

170. 1916

171. Mr. T

172. 6′3″

173. The threat by the Latvian Minister to Washington to declare war on the Russians if the Red Army took over his country

174. Her petticoat was falling down

175. 1945

176. What caused the roof of the Knickerbocker Theater to cave in and kill 90 persons in 1922?

177. About how many people work on Capitol Hill for Congresspersons and the Federal Government?

178. Which President reversed the order of his first and middle names?

179. Name the Washingtonian who wrote *Little Lord Fauntleroy*

180. Which was the capital's first equestrian statue?

181. Under what name did Soviet Foreign Minister Molotov slip into Washington in 1942?

182. Which current U.S. Senator won the Congressional Medal of Honor in Vietnam?

183. Which devout Mayor of Georgetown bought slaves to free them once they'd learned a trade?

184. What gift did President Kennedy's family make to the White House in his memory?

ANSWERS

176. A heavy snowstorm

177. 23,000

178. Dwight David Eisenhower

179. Mrs. Frances Hodgson Burnett

180. Andrew Jackson's, in Lafayette Square

181. Mr. Brown

182. Sen. Bob Kerrey (D-Nebraska)

183. Henry Foxall

184. Claude Monet's painting, *Matinée sur la Seine, beau temps*

185. He was a mining engineer who had worked in Australian gold fields and also in China, England, New Zealand, Burma and Russia before his election as U.S. President

186. In which historic home did Robert E. Lee refuse command of the Union Armies?

187. Which portfolio was given to Frances Perkins when she became the first female cabinet member in 1933?

188. How many rooms did real estate developer Morris Cafritz have in his Foxhall Road mansion?

189. Which is the Marriott flagship hotel?

190. Who is "Slava"?

191. When was the last streetcar removed from service in the capital?

192. Which President tried to leave Washington by boat on the inauguration day of his successor, only to find the skipper sailing away, shouting: "Ex-President—be dashed! Let him stay!"?

ANSWERS

185. Herbert Hoover

186. Blair House

187. Secretary of Labor

188. 58

189. The J. W. Marriott, corner 14th St. & Pennsylvania Avenue N.W.

190. Mstislav Rostropovich, Music Director of the National Symphony Orchestra

191. 1962

192. John Tyler

193. Where can you see a residential fence made of spiked gun barrels from the Mexican-American War of 1848?

194. Who furnished the State Department Diplomatic Reception Rooms into one of the finest collections of Americana?

195. Of what substance is the Vice-President's senatorial gavel made?

196. Over how many acres does the Washington Convention Center spread?

197. How thick are the walls at the base of the Washington Monument?

198. Where is live ammunition fired regularly within half a mile of the White House?

199. Where is the original Star-Spangled Banner which inspired the National Anthem?

200. How heavy are the bronze doors at the Constitution Avenue entrance to the National Archives?

201. What is the official name of Washington Cathedral?

202. What is *The Conference Handshake?*

ANSWERS

193. Outside 1516–18 28th St. N.W.

194. Clement E. Conger, Curator

195. Ivory

196. 9.7

197. 15 feet

198. Special agents have an indoor target range in the FBI building

199. In the National Museum of American History

200. 6½ tons each

201. The Cathedral Church of Saint Peter and Saint Paul

202. The traditional handshake Supreme Court Justices give each other before sitting on the bench or arriving at decisions

203. What are the colors and design of the District of Columbia flag?

204. Where can you see an international collection of the highest military honors?

205. Where do you register copyright?

206. Which bells are rung on the opening and closing of Congress?

207. Where is the oldest public aquarium in the USA?

208. Rarely seen without a carnation in his lapel, this Chief Executive called it his "good-luck charm"

209. When did the Chinese community move to present-day Chinatown?

210. This American composer's *Mass* was premiered at the opening of the Kennedy Center

211. Which Cabinet officer has responsibility for the Secret Service?

ANSWERS

203. A rectangular white background with two horizontal red bars, and three red stars in the upper white space

204. In the Trophy Room of the Memorial Amphitheater, Arlington National Cemetery

205. At the Library of Congress

206. The Congress Bells in the Old Post Office Building

207. In the basement of the Department of Commerce building

208. William McKinley

209. 1932

210. Leonard Bernstein

211. The Secretary of the Treasury

212. Which women's club is housed in the mansion where President Coolidge hosted Charles Lindbergh to tea?

213. Who was Speaker of the House of Representatives longer than any other person?

214. Where did Commodore Stephen Decatur die of wounds from a duel?

215. Who was the youngest man ever to *serve* as President?

216. Who was the youngest man ever *elected* President?

217. Guess the total number of Smithsonian Institution specimens and artifacts

218. Where does Washington rank among the nation's largest metropolitan areas?

219. How much did Eugene Meyer pay for *The Washington Post* in a 1933 auction sale?

220. Pope Pius IX commissioned him to restore the frescoes of Raphael's Loggia in the Vatican long before he emigrated to America to earn greater fame as decorator of the Capitol. Who was he?

ANSWERS

212. The Washington Club

213. Sam Rayburn of Texas

214. In the basement of his house on Lafayette Square

215. Theodore Roosevelt

216. John Kennedy

217. More than 100 million

218. Seventh

219. $825,000

220. Constantino Brumidi

221. What was so unusual about the cards placed on tables in pre-World War II Scholl's Cafeteria?

222. Where did President Madison live after the British burned the White House?

223. What job description entitles you to live at 801 G St. of Square 927 in Southeast Washington?

224. What killed *Redskins'* coach Vince Lombardi at age 57?

225. How was James Smithson's $500,000 bequest to the Smithsonian Institution shipped across the Atlantic Ocean?

226. Who is the largest employer in the District of Columbia?

227. What was the call sign of the airliner which brought Pope John Paul II to Andrews Air Force Base in 1979?

228. From what room of the Howard Johnson's Motor Lodge did a conspirator spy to warn Watergate buggers of impending danger?

229. What are the Columbus Doors?

ANSWERS

221. The message invited patrons to ask God's blessing on the meal

222. The Octagon House

223. Commandant of the U.S. Marine Corps

224. Cancer

225. In sackfulls of gold sovereigns filling 11 boxes

226. The Federal Government

227. *Shepherd One*

228. Room 723

229. Doors with sculptured scenes from the life of Christopher Columbus, in the Capitol

230. There are so many of them in metropolitan Washington that they number almost 1 of every 100 residents

231. The 23rd President was the grandson of the 9th President and the great-grandson of a signatory to the Declaration of Independence. Who was he?

232. How many convicted Nazi saboteurs were electrocuted in Washington on August 8, 1942?

233. Where were the Pisner quints born?

234. How many sons does Supreme Court Associate Justice Sandra Day O'Connor have?

235. Why did Charles Guiteau pay an extra dollar for the pistol he used to assassinate President Garfield?

236. How many rooms and baths did the White House have
    a. before
    b. after renovations were completed in 1952?

237. What is so odd about the leg bone on view at the Armed Forces Medical Museum?

ANSWERS

230. Lawyers

231. Benjamin Harrison

232. Six

233. George Washington University Hospital

234. Three

235. He believed that the bone, instead of a wooden handle, would look more impressive in a museum showcase

236. a. 62 rooms and 14 baths
    b. 132 rooms and 20 baths and showers

237. It was donated by the amputee, Major General Daniel Sickles, who had it blown off at the Battle of Gettysburg

238. When were U.S. Senate proceedings first televised?

239. Which local radio station beat out all other U.S. broadcasters in being the first to play a Beatles' record?

240. What is the total length of corridors in the Pentagon?

241. Where is the statue of Charles Carroll, the last surviving signatory to the Declaration of Independence?

242. Who was called "the daughter of the nation"?

243. Why did Watergate Special Prosecutor Leon Jaworski find it hard to concentrate in church on September 8, 1974?

244. What was the distance covered by John Riggins in setting a Super Bowl record of longest touchdown run from scrimmage?

245. Whose Georgetown home did Jacqueline Kennedy move into after the President's assassination?

246. Which great orator called Washington "Great Dismal"?

ANSWERS

238. 1986

239. WWDC

240. 17½ miles

241. In Statuary Hall inside the Capitol

242. Nellie Grant, daughter of President Ulysses J. Grant

243. He knew that President Ford was at that hour announcing a pardon for Richard Nixon

244. 43 yards

245. Averell Harriman's

246. Daniel Webster

247. In what year did suffragettes stage their largest demonstration in Washington?

248. Which photographer got closer to President Reagan than anyone else during the 1981 swearing-in ceremony?

249. Reputed to be the top lobbyist in Washington, his mother is a Congresswoman, as was his late father. Who is he?

250. What do the statues on each of the four corners of Lafayette Park have in common?

251. Who financed the founding in Georgetown of the Volta Bureau to aid the deaf?

252. What was so significant about the president of Georgetown University 1874–82?

253. How many persons can the Washington Convention Center accommodate?

254. Who was "Fishbait"?

255. What can you see in the Capitol crypt site originally set aside for George Washington's tomb?

ANSWERS

247. 1913

248. Senator Howard Baker

249. Thomas Hales Boggs Jr.

250. Kosciuszko, Rochambeau, Von Steuben and Lafayette were all foreigners who helped the American colonists

251. Alexander Graham Bell

252. Patrick J. Healy S.J. was the first black to head a major white university

253. 26,000

254. William Miller—Doorkeeper to the House of Representatives for 28 years

255. The catafalque on which deceased Presidents lay in state

256. What was the most fashionable street for embassies before they favored Massachusetts Avenue?

257. Why did diminutive Ethiopian Emperor Haile Selassie refuse to sleep in a 4-poster bed during a visit to Washington?

258. Where is the statue of Puck?

259. Long before his resignation from the Supreme Court, Abe Fortas was a founding partner of this legal firm

260. What physical impediment afflicts the czar of downtown property development?

261. Which Washington *Senators* pitcher shut out the New York *Yankees* in 3 successive games in 4 days?

262. In how many cities did George and Barbara Bush live between their marriage and move to the White House?

263. Which President swam in the White House pool with his glasses on?

264. Who edited the words carved into the frieze of the Post Office adjacent to Union Station?

ANSWERS

256. 16th St. N.W.

257. He complained it was too large

258. Outside the Folger Shakespeare Library

259. Arnold & Porter

260. Oliver Carr has been blind in one eye since birth

261. Walter Johnson

262. 17

263. Harry Truman

264. President Woodrow Wilson

265. Which President escaped assassination when both pistols of an insane Georgetown painter malfunctioned?

266. Where can you view the tallest Corinthian columns ever raised?

267. From where did Martin Luther King Jr. proclaim the words: "I have a dream"?

268. How many years did the *Washington Star* appear before folding?

269. What do the following have in common: Charles Drew, the discoverer of blood plasma, and Edward Brooke, the first black U.S. Senator since Reconstruction?

270. What is the minimum age requirement to be a member of Congress?

271. Where was poet Ezra Pound confined after being found mentally unfit to stand trial for treason during World War II?

272. The Renwick gallery was built to house which man's art collection?

273. Which First Ladies died during their husband's terms of office?

ANSWERS

265. Andrew Jackson

266. The eight 75 ft. columns are in the National Building Museum, Judiciary Square N.W.

267. The Lincoln Memorial

268. 128

269. They both attended Dunbar High School, the nation's first black high school

270. 30 for the Senate, 25 for the House

271. St. Elizabeth's Hospital, Washington, D.C.

272. William Wilson Corcoran

273. Letitia Tyler; Caroline Harrison; Ellen Wilson

274. Who starred in *The Little Foxes* at the Kennedy Center?

275. Why did Calvin Coolidge worship in the Metropolitan Theater in the mornings and at the 8th St. Synagogue in the evenings?

276. Of all the trees planted in the White House grounds, which is the oldest surviving one?

277. What historic discovery was made from the old U.S. Naval Observatory at Foggy Bottom in 1877?

278. Where will you find a bronze statue of Esther Morris of Wyoming—the first female justice of the peace?

279. Who was the most illustrious clerk in the Indian Bureau of the Department of the Interior?

280. Name the three Presidents who died on the Fourth of July

281. How did the British Ambassador dismiss criticism that *only* 1300 invitations were sent out for a garden party honoring the visiting King and Queen?

282. Who was "Uncle Joe"

ANSWERS

274. Elizabeth Taylor

275. These were temporary meeting places for members of the First Congregational Church of Washington while their church was closed for remodeling

276. An American Elm, planted in the 1820s by John Quincy Adams

277. The discovery of Deimos and Phobos, satellites of Mars

278. In Statuary Hall, inside the Capitol

279. Walt Whitman

280. John Adams, Thomas Jefferson, James Monroe

281. "It's just like heaven," he said. "Some are chosen, some are not!"

282. House Speaker Joseph Cannon

283. Who were known as "sundowners" at the turn of 19th century Washington?

284. Only these two Capitol Hill employees are empowered to arrest the President

285. Name the billionaire who began with a root beer soda fountain at 14th Street & Park Road N.W. in 1927

286. Name the Congressional Budget Office employee who became a hero during the Air Florida crash into the Potomac River

287. Which President married a woman whose guardian he had been since she was 11 years old?

288. This man outranked George Washington when Congress promoted him to 4-star General of the Army in 1866

289. Which U.S. Attorney for the District of Columbia became a household name after writing a brief piece of creative literature?

290. What disaster upon the Potomac River in 1884 took the lives of the Secretary of State and the Secretary of the Navy?

291. Which top Presidential aide drowned aboard the *Titanic*?

ANSWERS

283. Government employees who worked for themselves during and after office hours

284. The U.S. Senate Sergeant-at-Arms and his deputy

285. J. Willard Marriott

286. Lenny Skutnik

287. Grover Cleveland

288. Ulysses S. Grant

289. Francis Scott Key, who wrote *The Star Spangled Banner*

290. A cannon exploded aboard the *U.S.S. Princeton* during ceremonial firings

291. Archie Butt, personal aide to Theodore Roosevelt and then to William Howard Taft

292. Who were Emily, Lady Nashville and Bolivia?

293. In what year did the Washington *Senators* play their last baseball game before moving to Texas?

294. Columnist Joseph Alsop was a cousin of this President

295. Who was Maud Shaw?

296. Why was a former president of the Cleveland *Indians* refused service in the posh Sheraton-Carlton Hotel dining room?

297. What was the nightly pay for a driver liquor-running from southern Maryland to Washington during Prohibition?

298. Why was Mamie Eisenhower's favorite White House room the Red Room?

299. Who was the "Coonskin" Congressman?

300. What was the name of the comedy Abraham Lincoln was watching as he was assassinated?

301. What building has three times as much office space as the Empire State building in New York City?

ANSWERS

292. Racing fillies owned by President Andrew Jackson

293. 1971

294. Franklin Roosevelt

295. Caroline and John Kennedy Jr.'s White House English nannie

296. He refused to bow to the rule that men wear ties and jackets

297. $50 a night

298. Because she held her first reception there and said "there is something special about a first"

299. Davy Crockett

300. *Our American Cousin*

301. The Pentagon

302. Which famous author was a nurse in the Union Hospital at Georgetown during the Civil War?

303. In which year were theaters and movie houses integrated in D.C.?

304. Name the former player/manager of the Washington *Senators* who was elected to the Hall of Fame in 1956

305. When was slavery abolished in the District of Columbia?

306. Who sent a note to his Cabinet which read: "I am to be married on Wednesday evening at seven o'clock at the White House to Miss Folsom. It will be a very quiet affair and I will be extremely gratified at your attendance on this occasion"?

307. What gold charm did Katharine Graham wear on a chain around her neck as the *Washington Post* exposed the Watergate scandal?

308. Which wars are represented by a Tomb of the Unknown Soldier at Arlington National Cemetery?

ANSWERS

302. Louisa Alcott

303. 1953

304. Joseph Edward Cronin

305. 1862

306. Grover Cleveland

307. A gold wringer with rollers and handle, resembling parts of old-fashioned washing machines

308. World Wars I & II, The Korean War and the Vietnam War

309. What is known among the Washington legal fraternity as C & B?

310. Of what wood are legislators' desks made in the U.S. Senate?

311. Which Presidents signed the U.S. Constitution?

312. Why did aging politicians flock to Duncanson Brothers' auction rooms a century ago?

313. Where were Lyndon and Lady Bird Johnson living before moving to the White House?

314. What did the Kennedys arrange for after-dinner entertainment when they invited Nobel Prizewinners to the White House?

315. Which famous landmark had to have its foundations enlarged and strengthened for fear the whole structure would collapse when finally finished?

316. On what occasion did the U.S. Marine Band play *The Eyes of Texas* in the Rayburn House Office building?

317. Where was President Garfield mortally wounded by an assassin?

ANSWERS

309. The legal firm of Covington & Burling

310. Mahogany

311. George Washington and James Madison

312. To buy coffins

313. The Elms, 4040 52nd St. N.W.

314. Frederic March read unpublished works of Nobel Prizewinner Ernest Hemingway

315. The Washington Monument

316. At the dedication of the Sam Rayburn statue

317. In the waiting room of the Baltimore & Potomac Railroad Station, then at 6th & B Streets

QUESTIONS

318. Which First Lady was known as "Lemonade Lucy"?

319. Who was the first monarch to visit the capital?

320. What is the capital's leading private industry?

321. President Reagan read this novel by his favorite author while hospitalized for his colon operation

322. Where is Thomas Jefferson's original rough draft of the Declaration of Independence?

323. Who was honored at the first public gathering of women members of the District of Columbia bar in 1917?

324. What is the oldest Potomac River bridge in the Washington area?

325. What name was given to the temporary dwellings put up on the Mall and Parks during the poor people's march in 1968?

326. Which local cartoonist has won 3 Pulitzer Prizes?

327. Who said: "Our long national nightmare is over"?

ANSWERS

318. Mrs. Rutherford Hayes—after the water she
     served at White House dinners and the weak
     punch offered at receptions

319. King David Kalakaua of the Hawaiian
     Islands

320. Tourism

321. *Jubal Sackett* by Louis L'Amour

322. In the Library of Congress

323. Four men who had participated in a suffrage
     parade 4 years earlier

324. Chain Bridge at Little Falls

325. Resurrection City

326. The *Washington Post's* Herbert "Herblock"
     Block

327. President Ford, after taking office

328. Invited to address Congress in 1941, this foreign leader told legislators: "If my father had been an American and my mother British, instead of the other way round, I might have got here on my own"

329. Where is the largest Catholic Church in America?

330. What was the trade of Foster Shannon, father of the half of Shannon & Luchs?

331. Name the wealthy Washington brewer who died aged 102

332. Why is Somerset Maugham's book manuscript, *The Artistic Temperament of Stephen Carey* lying unpublished in the Library of Congress?

333. What is the second largest tributary of the larger Chesapeake Bay system?

334. Who was the first President inaugurated in Washington D.C.?

335. If you look out of the De Sales Street side of the Mayflower Hotel, which TV network's offices will you see?

ANSWERS

328. Winston Churchill

329. The National Shrine of the Immaculate Conception at 4th St. & Michigan Ave. N.E.

330. Carpentry

331. Christian Heurich

332. Maugham wrote it as the first version of the bestseller *Of Human Bondage* and donated it to the Library of Congress conditional on its not being published

333. The Potomac River

334. Thomas Jefferson

335. ABC

336. In which book did Carter press secretary, Jody Powell, savage journalistic luminaries?

337. How much did it cost Thomas Walsh to build his 60-room mansion at 2020 Massachusetts Avenue N.W. in 1903 (now the Indonesian Embassy)?

338. Name the famous singer/showman son of Washington Rabbi Morris Yoelson

339. Who was the first 20th century Mayor of Washington?

340. Why were balloons flown over the Potomac swamps in 1861?

341. Which Secretary of Defense was the son of a wholesale shoe firm's sales manager?

342. Whom did the Washington *Bullets* beat in 1978 to win the NBA crown?

343. Who described his job of Vice President as "the spare tire in our government"?

ANSWERS

336. *The Other Side Of The Story*

337. $835,000

338. Al Jolson

339. Walter Washington

340. The chief of the Aeronautic Service, Balloon Corps, experimented to observe Confederates, who in turn tried to shoot them down with artillery shells

341. Robert McNamara

342. The Seattle *Supersonics*

343. John Nance Garner

344. Select the correct total (rounded out to the nearest million) assessed value of Washington D.C. property in 1900
a. $11 million
b. $177 million
c. $429 million

345. Which President said: "I am not worried about my enemies; it is my friends that are keeping me awake nights"?

346. Where can you view fragments of Abraham Lincoln's skull?

347. How many Mormons live in the Washington area?

348. What same implement was used at ground-breaking ceremonies for The Lincoln Memorial, The Jefferson Memorial and The Kennedy Center?

349. Who was the first President to welcome a Pope to the White House?

350. How was aviator George Bush rescued after parachuting into the Pacific following a World War II bombing raid?

ANSWERS

344. b.

345. Warren Harding

346. In the Armed Forces Medical Museum at Walter Reed Army Medical Center

347. 35,000

348. A gold-plated shovel

349. Jimmy Carter

350. By a U.S. submarine

351. At what hour of the morning were five men arrested while breaking into Democratic Party headquarters in the Watergate?

352. How many square feet make up the largest of Giant's 132 supermarkets?

353. What is the best-known dish on the Senate restaurant menu?

354. Name the first Jewess elected to Congress

355. What is the oldest public building in continuous use in the nation's capital?

356. Why did President Coolidge remove a saucer from under his cup and fill it with cream during a State dinner?

357. What was the Indian name for the area that became the Federal capital?

358. Why did a bell rope break in St. John's Church, Lafayette Square, on August 14, 1945?

359. What was unique about President Kennedy's Lincoln Continental?

ANSWERS

351. 2:30 a.m.

352. 60,000 square feet—in Rockville, Md.

353. Bean soup

354. Florence Prag Kahn (R.-Calif.) 1925

355. The home of the Marine Corps Commandant

356. To feed the cat on the floor

357. Conococheague

358. It had been pulled without a break for three hours to celebrate victory over Japan

359. The power-operated back seat could be raised 10½" when the rear roof was removed

360. Spanish cellist Pablo Casals first performed at the White House in 1904. When was his next performance there?

361. Which museum has a theater with a screen 50 ft. high and 75 ft. wide?

362. Whose ashes are buried in the Rose Garden of Dumbarton Oaks?

363. How long did it take to sell the 52,000 tickets to the Bruce Springsteen concert in Washington in 1985?

364. Where is the downtown house of Mary Eugenia Surratt, the first woman hanged in the USA as a conspirator in the Lincoln assassination?

365. How many guests were invited to dine with visiting Princess Elizabeth and Prince Philip of Britain when they visited the Trumans in 1951?

366. After whom does the Chief Justice rank according to protocol?

367. On which monument are some words misspelled and other words missing from quotations from the Declaration of Independence?

ANSWERS

360. 1961

361. The National Air & Space Museum

362. Mr. & Mrs. Robert Woods Bliss, former owners of the Georgetown mansion

363. 90 minutes

364. 604 H. St. N.W.

365. 18

366. After the President, Vice President and Speaker of the House of Representatives

367. The Jefferson Memorial. Compared with the original document, misspelled words are *unalienable* and *honor*. Words dropped from quoted sentences include "...unalienable Rights, *that* among...."; "...that these *United* Colonies...."; and "....pledge *to each other* our lives...."

368. Which publication reports Congressional proceedings verbatim?

369. Where can you see the largest number of pre-Civil War buildings between Capitol Hill and Georgetown?

370. Which 62-year-old diplomat fell in love with a 16-year-old blond schoolgirl at a Georgetown Christmas party, then married her?

371. How long did it take for the first steamboat on the Potomac to reach Washington from New York?

372. To whom did Henry Kissinger dedicate *White House Years*?

373. This Washington socialite was daughter-in-law of a British Prime Minister before her marriage to a multi-millionaire Democrat

374. During an illustrious career in the military, this longtime Washington resident wrote *The Uncertain Trumpet*. Who was he?

375. Who was the first American to give his private art collection to the nation, together with a showpiece building and an endowment for its support?

ANSWERS

368. Congressional Record

369. In Chinatown

370. Baron Alexander de Bodisco, Czarist Minister to the U.S.

371. 50 hours

372. Nelson A. Rockefeller

373. Pamela (Churchill) Harriman

374. General Maxwell Taylor

375. Charles Lang Freer

376. Name the first gas company chartered by Congress

377. Where is the only astronomical observatory in the USA that determines time?

378. Which underground passages leading from the White House have long been sealed?

379. When did a U.S. President first appear on television?

380. Alone among 20th century U.S. Presidents, this one did not attend college

381. How many Regents govern the Smithsonian Institution?

382. What was the name of the British Admiral who ordered Washington burned in 1814?

383. Why was the historic home in Georgetown of Francis Scott Key destroyed?

384. What was the fate of President Garfield's assassin?

385. Which restaurant frequently offers rattlesnake steaks?

ANSWERS

376. The Washington Gas Light Company

377. The Naval Observatory grounds on Massachusetts Avenue N.W.

378. Those leading to the Octagon House

379. Franklin Roosevelt at the World's Fair, N.Y. 1939

380. Harry Truman

381. 17

382. Sir George Cockburn

383. To make way for a ramp for the Whitehurst Freeway

384. Charles Guiteau was hanged in the District Jail in 1882

385. Dominique's

386. When was RFK stadium completed?

387. How much was spent on redoing the living quarters for the Reagan's move into the White House?

388. What tragic event made Mary Todd Lincoln vow never again to enter the Green Room of the White House?

389. Why did baseball fans at RFK Stadium hold up signs like "We've been Short-changed" in 1971?

390. What is the real first name of Lady Bird Johnson?

391. In whose administration were women given the vote?

392. Why is composer Igor Stravinsky's *Concerto in E Flat* known as the *Dumbarton Oaks Concerto?*

393. Whose estate became part of Arlington National Cemetery?

394. Where is the only painting in America by Leonardo da Vinci?

ANSWERS

386. 1961

387. $730,000

388. It was in this room that her son, Willie, 11, was prepared for burial after dying of typhoid fever

389. Because Washington *Senators'* owner, Bob Short, moved the team to Texas

390. Claudia

391. Woodrow Wilson's

392. It was first performed at Dumbarton Oaks, the home of the couple who commissioned it

393. Confederate leader Robert E. Lee

394. In the National Gallery of Art

395. Which contralto was barred by the Daughters of the American Revolution from singing in Constitution Hall because she was black?

396. Who told his physician with eerie accuracy: "In two days I shall be a dead man"?

397. Why did Sherman Adams resign as President Eisenhower's close adviser?

398. Who grossed more than $2 million from her play *The Women* before serving two terms as a Congresswoman?

399. How did Sugar Ray Leonard become WBC World Welterweight Boxing Champ?

400. Name the four U.S. Presidents who were left-handed

401. How did Smithsonian officials justify a private evening tour of the Museum of American History for Michael Jackson?

402. Which historian and chronicler of the Kennedy administration was thrown fully clothed into a swimming pool at a Washington suburban party?

ANSWERS

395. Marian Anderson

396. President Zachary Taylor, during an attack of cholera

397. Because he received gifts, including a $700 vicuna coat, from a businessman on whose behalf he interceded with Federal regulatory agencies

398. Clare Boothe Luce

399. By a TKO in the 15th round against Wilfredo Benitez

400. Garfield, Truman, Ford, Bush

401. A spokesman said ''he is a citizen who cannot see what the museum has to offer during the regular hours.''

402. Arthur Schlesinger Jr.

403. Guess how much U.S. Senators were paid each day the Senate was in session in 1789

404. What does the acronym COPS stand for?

405. Which fancy women's club is housed in a mansion named after George Washington's ancestral home in England?

406. Which President insisted on paying $50 a year to rent a pew in the Presbyterian Church on New York Avenue & H. Street N.W.?

407. Pope Pius XI called this Washington institution "the Alma Mater of all Catholic colleges in the United States."

408. Which President became the first American to be awarded the Nobel Prize for Peace?

409. General Sherman denounced this building as, "The worst of it is, it is fireproof"

410. Where is the grave of John Howard Payne, author of *Home, Sweet Home?*

411. Does the Tourmobile sightseeing operation have an exclusive or monopolistic right to provide the tourist shuttle service along its routes?

ANSWERS

403. $6 per day

404. Chief of Operations (in the Directorate of Plans, CIA)

405. The Sulgrave

406. Abraham Lincoln

407. Georgetown University, founded in 1789

408. Theodore Roosevelt

409. The Pension Building

410. Oak Hill Cemetery, Georgetown

411. No. The National Park Service granted it only a "preferential right"

412. Which building named for a President has more space than 35 football fields?

413. What is the seating capacity of RFK Stadium?

414. Why were Women's Auxiliary Army Corps (WAAC) caps known as *Hobby caps*?

415. Where was President Reagan shot?

416. For how long was George Bush the first official "acting President" during Ronald Reagan's surgery in 1985?

417. What is unique about Joan of Ark's statue in Meridian Hill Park?

418. How much did Joe Allbritton
a. pay for the *Washington Star* in 1974
b. sell it for to *Time* Inc. in 1978?

419. What memorial to a 20th century President was once known as My Lord's Island?

420. What Capitol Hill figure has survived numerous strikes by lightning?

421. Why did a Supreme Court Justice fear he would look like a beetle?

ANSWERS

412. The James Madison Memorial Building of the Library of Congress

413. 55,363

414. After WAAC commander, Major Oveta Culp Hobby

415. Outside the Washington Hilton Hotel

416. 7 hours 56 minutes

417. It is the only equestrian statue of a woman in D.C.

418. a. $35 million
    b. $20 million

419. Theodore Roosevelt Island

420. *Freedom*—the 19 ft. high statue of a female standing above the Capitol dome and grounded by lightning rods on the shoulders and headdress

421. Because the Supreme Court building was so large when finished in 1935 that he quipped: "We will look like nine black beetles in the Temple of Karnak"

422. For what reason is the Social List of Washington D.C. — the directory of socially prominent people — known as "the Green Book"?

423. Who led the CIA team which gave the White House the first photographs showing missile sites under construction in Cuba?

424. After what perennial plants are the cabins and lodges named at Camp David?

425. Better known as the inventor of the punched tabulating card, Herman Hollerith is also remembered for designing his Georgetown mansion like a factory — to deceive who?

426. They made such a racket that employees banished them from the headquarters of the Organization of American States. Who were they?

427. Why did President Buchanan sleep on a sofa in a hall of the White House?

428. The father of veteran UPI White House correspondent, Helen Thomas, immigrated from this Middle Eastern country

ANSWERS

422. It has a green cover

423. Dr. Ray Cline, then a Deputy Director of the CIA

424. Trees

425. The tax assessor

426. Macaws and toucans—tropical birds who were delivered to the National Zoo

427. In 1860 he offered his bedroom to the visiting Prince of Wales, son of Queen Victoria

428. Lebanon

429. Which Senate Majority Leader wrote: "Photography has gradually become the way I keep my diary"?

430. How many acres comprise Washington Dulles International Airport?

431. This Navy pilot, in Vietnamese captivity for almost 9 years, later became deputy head of the Peace Corps and then of the Veterans Administration

432. What is The Old Guard?

433. When was the Hechinger Company founded?

434. Which dog wrote his autobiography during the Reagan administration?

435. What popular Christmastime tradition was initiated by Pat Nixon?

436. How did Kathryn Seller make legal history in 1918?

437 Which diplomatic head of mission was handcuffed by an Elkton, Md. constable for resisting arrest on a charge of speeding?

438. What is the total acreage of Anacostia Park?

ANSWERS

429. Howard Baker

430. 10,943

431. Everett Alvarez

432. The Army honor guard which performs at ceremonial functions

433. 1911

434. C. Fred Bush, with editorial help from Barbara Bush, wife of the Vice President

435. Candlelight tours of the White House

436. Her appointment to the D.C. Bench (Juvenile Court) made her the first woman judge under Federal authority

437. An Iranian (1936)

438. 750 acres

439. Who was "Mister Sam"?

440. After whom was Georgetown named?

441. What was the largest jackpot prize given by a local radio station?

442. How old was Sugar Ray Leonard when his family moved from South Carolina to Washington D.C.?

443. About how many fans showed up for the downtown parade to honor the Super Bowl XVII victors?

444. Who holds the record for the most Presidential news conferences?

445. What did the Franklin Mint, Philadelphia give to the State Department as a Bicentennial gift?

446. Why did Representative Daniel Sickles (D.-N.Y.) shoot to death the son of Francis Scott Key?

447. Under which roof can you view the court robes worn by Judge John Sirica of Watergate fame?

ANSWERS

439. House Speaker Sam Rayburn

440. George Boone, an Englishman, who bought land in the neighborhood

441. $1 million by WASH-FM in 1984

442. Four years old

443. An estimated 500,000

444. Franklin Roosevelt held 998 in 12 years

445. A pastel portrait of Benjamin Franklin, drawn from life in 1777 (on view in the Jefferson State Reception Room)

446. He found out that Key was having an affair with the Congressman's wife

447. The National Museum of American History

448. The back of a $20 bill shows a pair of evergreen Southern Magnolias to the left of the South Portico of the White House. Who planted them in memory of his wife?

449. What historic appointment was made in 1970 regarding D.C. schools?

450. What is Washington sometimes disparagingly known as?

451. Name the Presidents who died in the following circumstances:

   a. Of a stroke in a San Francisco hotel, while his wife was reading an article about him entitled *A calm view of a calm man*

   b. In the bedroom of his home, after working outdoors planning a fish-pond, during a snowfall

   c. Of pneumonia, in bed in the White House

   d. Of cholera in bed in the White House, less than a week after complaining of the heat on the Fourth of July

   e. In bed at Elberon, N.J., two months after an assassin's bullet lodged behind his pancreas

ANSWERS

448. President Andrew Jackson, seen on the reverse side of the bill

449. A black was appointed Superintendent of D.C. Schools for the first time

450. "The gas house of the nation"

451. a. Warren Harding
     b. George Washington
     c. William Henry Harrison
     d. Zachary Taylor
     e. James Garfield

f. In bed at Buffalo, N.Y., from gunshot wounds inflicted by an assassin concealing a pistol in a bandaged hand

g. Of a cerebral hemorrhage a few hours after being sketched by a portrait artist at Warm Springs, Ga.

452. How many invitations did the Chinese send out for the World War II visit to Washington of Madame Chiang Kai-Shek?

453. What is the highest point in Washington D.C.?

454. How many acres of the U.S. Naval Observatory grounds are given over to the Vice President for his official home?

455. How much did Imasco, the Canadian food and tobacco conglomerate, pay for the Peoples Drug Stores chain in 1984?

456. What closely-guarded temporary structures were placed on the Potomac River in World War II?

457. Why was Teddy Roosevelt compared to a grasshopper?

ANSWERS

451. f. William McKinley
   g. Franklin Roosevelt

452. 3,000

453. The pinnacle of the Gloria in Excelsis tower of Washington Cathedral, at 676 ft. above sea level

454. 10

455. $320 million

456. Two wooden bridges supported by pontoons, crossing from the bottom of Wisconsin Avenue & 14th Streets N.W.

457. "Because," went the popular reply, "you never know which way he'll hop, but when he does, he'll hop like hell"

458. How did Mt. Vernon get its name?

459. Which ancient Greek is quoted on the frieze along the length of the Constitution Avenue side of the National Academy of Sciences?

460. Which Washington legal firm is the only one ranked among the National Law Journal's 50 largest in the country?

461. Where was the location of the old Shoreham Hotel for four decades?

462. Who were code-named *Hertz* and *Avis* by Spiro Agnew's staff?

463. When Robert McNamara was Secretary of Defense he used a 60-drawer desk which once belonged to this famous World War I general

464. What occasion did John Philip Sousa pick to make his last public appearance as a conductor?

465. Who opened fire with pistols in the House of Representatives, wounding five Congresspersons in 1954?

466. This 133 ft. former mobile lighthouse is moored off Hains Point in the Washington Channel

ANSWERS

458. Before bequeathing the property to his brother George, Lewis Washington named it in honor of British Admiral Edward Vernon

459. Aristotle

460. Covington & Burling

461. On the northwest corner of 15th & H. Streets N.W.

462. Nixon was *Hertz* and Agnew was *Avis*

463. General John Pershing

464. The Bicentennial celebrations of George Washington's birthday

465. Puerto Rican nationalists

466. Lighthouse Chesapeake

467. What was the score in the 7th game of the final playoff round which gave the Washington *Bullets* the NBA championship in 1978?

468. Who was the first woman to practice before the Supreme Court?

469. Which U.S. senator from the Pacific Northwest was known as "the Lone Ranger" for frequently voting in the minority?

470. Where did Septimia Randolph Meikleham, last surviving grandchild of Thomas Jefferson, die?

471. Unsurpassed as a hostess of lavish parties, this Washington socialite was also Ambassador to Luxembourg

472. What was the name of Washington's earliest newspaper, which was also the first national newspaper?

473. If the statue at the Lincoln Memorial could stand up straight how tall would it be?

474. This Presidential pet was dressed in bright red boots and a red felt coat for a White House wedding

ANSWERS

467. *Bullets* 105, Seattle *Supersonics* 99

468. Mrs. Belva Lockwood

469. Wayne Morse (D-Ore.)

470. 1429 Q. Street N.W.

471. Perle Mesta

472. *The National Intelligencer*

473. 28 ft.

474. Lyndon Johnson's mongrel dog, Yuki

475. Where did Hains Point get its name from?

476. When did Washingtonians first take part in Presidential elections?

477. Whom did coach George Allen hire to try and improve the *Redskins* chances against Miami in Super Bowl VII?

478. Why did Senator John Calhoun of South Carolina want to reject the half million dollar gift from an Englishman to found the Smithsonian Institution?

479. When did Alexandria recede to Virginia?

480. Who bankrupted the city coffers with public works projects, then made a fortune in gold and silver in Mexico?

481. Why was National Airport allowed to be built so close to downtown Washington?

482. Which First Lady was the daughter of a former President's law partner, and then the wife of a President?

483. Why did the Santee Sioux Chief, Scarlet Crow, fail to return home after visiting Washington?

ANSWERS

475. Major Peter Hains of the U.S. Engineers, in charge of filling and dredging Potomac Parks

476. 1964

477. An expert to chart the angle of the sun over the Los Angeles stadium

478. He thought it "beneath the dignity of the United States to receive presents of this kind from anyone"

479. 1846

480. Alexander "Boss" Shepherd

481. Because the capital has no skyscrapers

482. Helen Taft

483. He was murdered in the capital

484. Which celebrated newspaper publisher asked: "Are comics important?"

485. How many attempts were made on the life of Charles Guiteau after he killed President Garfield?

486. What is the diameter of the largest telescope at the city's Naval Observatory?

487. When was the design accepted for the flag of the District of Columbia?

488. Which Washington wit coaxed: "If you don't have anything good to say about anybody, come sit beside me"

489. Why was Soviet diplomat Gennadi Fedorovich Mashkansev ordered out of Washington in 1957?

490. Who was the first journalist to be known as the "White House reporter"?

491. How tall was George Washington?

492. Where is the official residence of the Vice President?

ANSWERS

484. Eugene Meyer, on acquiring the *Washington Post*

485. Two

486. 26 inches

487. 1938

488. Alice Roosevelt Longworth

489. For pressuring a Soviet defector to return to the USSR

490. *Washington Star* staffer, William W. Price, in 1897

491. 6'2"

492. In Observatory Circle, Massachusetts Avenue N.W.

493. What does the motto *E. Pluribus Unum* (From many, one) refer to?

494. How many fatalities were there as a result of an Air Florida plane crashing into the Potomac River in 1982?

495. What was the 1983 maiden season record of the USFL *Washington Federals*?

496. What is the costliest building ever put up by the Public Buildings Service?

497. How long is the Potomac River?

498. Who ate in the White House and then set fire to it?

499. What was Richard Nixon's first inaugural parade theme?

500. An attempt to nickname this Rhodes Scholar "Senator Halfbright" never caught on

501. On what single occasion are flags allowed over graves at Arlington National Cemetery?

502. The palace of the Maharajah of Rewa in India supplied this rare animal to the Zoo

ANSWERS

493. The separate American colonies being combined into one nation

494. 74 passengers and crew and 4 others on the 14th Street bridge

495. 4-14

496. FBI headquarters

497. About 385 miles, of which 104 is tidewater (Little Falls to the Chesapeake Bay)

498. British officers during the invasion of 1814

499. *Forward Together*

500. Senator William Fulbright

501. Memorial Day

502. A white tiger

503. Who shot and mortally wounded former Kentucky Representative, William Preston Taulbee, on the Capitol staircase in 1890?

504. Which son of a President became Secretary of War and then Minister to England?

505. How did the Phillips Collection make art history?

506. Where do Congressional Pages attend school?

507. What did Ronald Reagan tell Jimmy Carter on their way to Reagan's inauguration?

508. Since the last century it has been traditional for ships and steamboats to do this whenever they pass Mt. Vernon

509. How much money is spent annually at D.C.'s eateries and drinking wells?

510. Name the princely son of a Middle Eastern monarch who attended St. Alban's School in the precincts of Washington Cathedral

511. What was the value of loot amassed by long-time burglar Bernard Welch before being nabbed in 1980?

ANSWERS

503. Charles Kincaid, Washington correspondent for the *Louisville Times*. The incident arose out of an article he had written, but the writer was acquitted

504. Robert Todd Lincoln

505. It was the first museum of modern art in the USA

506. Capitol Page School, Library of Congress, 10 1st St. S.E.

507. A couple of corny jokes, according to Carter

508. Toll their bells

509. Over $600 million

510. Prince Faisal, son of King Hussein of Jordan

511. Approximately $4 million

512. Which Secretary of State described himself as "your friendly neighborhood bartender"?

513. Better known as the founder of the American Red Cross, this person was also the first woman to be given an offical government appointment

514. Which Speaker of the House used to signal the end of a House term by playing his violin for Congressmen?

515. Which President escaped injury when plaster fell from the ceiling of the First Congregational Church during a Thanksgiving Day service?

516. What was the Capitol Rotunda used for during the Civil War?

517. Which club was founded in 1964 after the Cosmos Club denied membership to black journalist Carl Rowan?

518. Where is the statue of the only Congressperson to vote against U.S. entry into both World Wars?

519. What is Washington's most coveted invitation, excluding those from the White House?

ANSWERS

512. Dean Rusk

513. Clara Barton

514. Nicholas Longworth

515. Calvin Coolidge

516. A soldiers' barracks, then a hospital

517. The International Club

518. Jeannette Rankin's statue is in Statuary Hall in the Capitol

519. An invitation to the June Garden Party at the British Embassy in honor of the Queen's birthday

QUESTIONS

520. What did the new official residence of the Secretary of the Smithsonian cost the Institution when it bought the Cleveland Park mansion in 1984?

521. Why did the dancing have to stop when the First Lady arrived at the inaugural balls for President Polk?

522. How many Ku Klux Klansmen paraded in Washington in 1925?

523. Which is the oldest theater in the city?

524. At which club did Korean influence peddlar Tongsun Park entertain in lavish style?

525. Who was the most infamous actor ever to play Shakespeare's *Richard III* in Washington?

526. How many bulbs does the U.S. Park Service plant anew in the Washington area every year?

527. What is the origin of the name Anacostia?

528. Which Washington area real estate company has the highest value of assets?

ANSWERS

520. $485,000

521. First Lady Sarah Polk was an austere Calvinist who disapproved of dancing and other "vanities of the world"

522. 50,000

523. National Theater

524. The George Town Club

525. John Wilkes Booth, at Ford's Theater 17 months before he shot Abraham Lincoln

526. 570,000

527. It is the Latinized form of Nacochtank, a former Indian settlement in the same vicinity

528. The Rouse Company

529. What did Lady Bird Johnson admit was her favorite view of Washington?

530. This conservation-minded President said: "I hate a man who would skin the land"

531. Between which stations did the Metro Orange line train crash, with the loss of 3 lives in 1982?

532. Who administered the oath of office to Daniel Boorstin, Librarian of Congress?

533. Name the White House occupant who wrote: "May none but honest and wise men ever rule under this roof"

534. Why was telephone service momentarily discontinued nationwide in 1922?

535. What do all the Potomac bridges have in common?

536. How many species of birds would you find if you observed the District of Columbia area for a year?

537. Where will you find a reconstruction of an ancient Japanese tea house?

ANSWERS

529. Looking south over White House magnolias to the Washington Monument

530. Theodore Roosevelt

531. Federal Triangle and Smithsonian

532. Then Speaker of the House of Representatives, Carl Albert

533. President John Adams

534. As a tribute to the inventor of the telephone, Alexander Graham Bell, during his burial

535. No overhead construction

536. About 180

537. At the Japanese Embassy

538. Who promoted the first Muhammed Ali-Joe Frazier boxing clash?

539. When was an Air Express service inaugurated for mail between Washington and the West Coast?

540. What are the complete 21 words of Commodore Stephen Decatur's banquet toast, remembered only as "My Country—Right or Wrong!"

541. In which city was the founder of the Giant supermarkets born?

542. Though a U.S. President must be at least 35 and a natural-born citizen, how many years must he have lived in the USA?

543. How did Congressional Cemetery get its name?

544. A set of George Washington's false teeth were made from rhinoceros ivory, held together by spiral springs, stained with port wine and set in sealing wax to simulate gums. True or false?

545. Why is the State Department known as Foggy Bottom?

ANSWERS

538. Jack Kent Cooke

539. December 26, 1929

540. "Our country! In her intercourse with foreign nations, may she always be in the right; but our country—right or wrong!"

541. Jerusalem

542. 14 years

543. For many years Congressmen were buried there

544. True

545. Because of its bureaucratic methods and views

546. Explain why Jacqueline Kennedy played Santa Claus in 1961

547. The cornerstone of which building holds a copy of the Declaration of Independence, the New Testament, Congressional Directory of 1847, and a medal portrait of James Smithson?

548. Which is the oldest Catholic College in the U.S.?

549. Which street was once designated The Avenue of the Presidents?

550. How did the National Press Club justify waiving a penalty for late dues from President Franklin Roosevelt?

551. 1950 marked the desegregation of which public sports facilities in the capital?

552. Why did Sir Lionel Sackville-West lose his job as British Ambassador in Washington?

553. Which recent President never got the opportunity to nominate anyone to the Supreme Court?

ANSWERS

546. She gave out presents to patients at the District of Columbia Children's Hospital

547. The Smithsonian "Castle"

548. Georgetown University

549. 16th Street N.W.

550. He was out of town when the dues deadline expired

551. Swimming pools

552. He made the mistake of saying whom he preferred to win the U.S. election and compounded this gaffe by picking the loser, Grover Cleveland, instead of the victor, Benjamin Harrison

553. Jimmy Carter

554. Where is the memorial to Marion Ooletia Kahlert, 10, who in 1904 became the first casualty of a motor vehicle?

555. Where was President Reagan's limo speeding when he began coughing blood after the assassination attempt?

556. How did the *Redskins* get their name?

557. Who was *The Old Fox*?

558. Which black attended Takoma Elementary School, Paul Junior High, then St. Alban's School for Boys before winning a Rhodes Scholarship?

559. Why did Mississippi-born Marion Barry come to live in Washington?

560. How much did John Coleman spend on refurbishing and renovating the Ritz-Carlton Hotel soon after he bought it in 1977?

561. Rebecca Felton (Independent Democrat-Ga.) was the first woman appointed to the U.S. Senate. How long did she serve?

562. Which prized British decoration did President Eisenhower wear at a State Dinner for the Queen of England?

ANSWERS

554. Her statue stands over her grave in Congressional Cemetery

555. In the tunnel below Dupont Circle

556. It was a carryover from the *Boston Redskins* after the club moved from Boston to Washington

557. General Charles Cornwallis' nickname for George Washington, in tribute to his shrewd military judgment

558. Randall Kennedy

559. To head the Washington office of the Student Non-Violent Coordinating Committee

560. $7 million

561. One day. She was sworn in 7 weeks later but the following day made way for the newly-elected senator

562. The Order of Merit

563. Who was the long-time chairman of the Kennedy Center's Board of Trustees?

564. How much did the Daughters of the American Revolution pay for Constitution Hall and the land it is built upon?

565. What was it about the physical appearance of Senator Benjamin Ryan Tillman (D-S.C.) that made him different from his colleagues?

566. Who was the first Presidential bride to be married in the White House?

567. What name did sculptor Thomas Crawford give to his bronze statue above the dome of the Capitol?

568. A drunken bricklayer who beat his wife to death was the first man hanged in Washington—during Jefferson's administration. Where were the gallows?

569. Why did Secretary of State Dean Rusk refuse to put a telephone in the bedroom of his Quebec Street home?

570. In a break with tradition, President Reagan's 1981 inauguration was held on which side of the Capitol?

ANSWERS

563. Roger Stevens

564. $1.57 million

565. He had a glass eye in his left socket

566. Frances Folsom, who married Grover Cleveland in 1886

567. *Freedom Triumphant*

568. At the foot of Capitol Hill, between Pensylvania and Maryland Avenues

569. So that he would have to walk across an adjoining hallway and be fully awake before lifting the receiver

570. The west

571. Name the giant pandas at the National Zoo

572. What local landmark was the tallest masonry structure in the world when completed in 1884?

573. How, according to protocol, do ambassadors rank one another?

574. What is the estimated number of worshippers who celebrated Mass on the Mall with Pope John Paul II?

575. What was so outstanding about the first black to buy property in Le Droit park?

576. Is it true that a Mitsubishi Zero Japanese naval fighter plane is within striking distance of the Capitol?

577. How did John Philip Sousa come to compose *The Washington Post March*?

578. When did Jacqueline Kennedy present her CBS televised tour of the White House?

579. Who borrowed a military sword to slice her wedding cake at a White House reception?

580. When was the Old Stone House built in Georgetown?

ANSWERS

571. Hsing-Hsing and Ling-Ling

572. The Washington Monument

573. According to length of continuous service in Washington

574. 175,000

575. Christian Fleetwood had won the Congressional Medal of Honor in the Civil War

576. Yes. This warplane, used in the attack on Pearl Harbor, is in the Air & Space Museum

577. The newspaper owners had asked him to compose a piece to publicize an essay contest they were sponsoring

578. February 1962

579. Alice Roosevelt Longworth

580. About 1765

581. Who was the most famous chronicler of early Washington society?

582. At what Georgetown address did John Kennedy live before moving to the White House?

583. Which President had a 19" neck?

584. Who is "Uncle Beazley"?

585. What were the statistics of the largest flag ever unfurled on the Mall on Flag Day?

586. Why was a gallant Englishman wheeled onto the floor of the House of Representatives at a joint meeting of Congress in 1943?

587. What deadly reptiles did a child steal from the Zoo, and were they recovered?

588. Where is the Washington memorial to Samuel Gompers, founder of the American Federation of Labor?

589. What racist incident marked the dedication of the Lincoln Memorial?

590. When was the Vice President's rostrum built in the U.S. Senate?

581. Margaret Bayard Smith

582. 3307 N. St.

583. William Howard Taft

584. The 22 ft. long fiber-glass reproduction of a prehistoric Triceratops, outside the Museum of Natural History

585. It covered about 2½ acres and measured 411 ft. × 211 ft.

586. Lt. Hon. Richard Wood, who lost both legs in action in North Africa, was the son of British Ambassador Lord Halifax, and had come to hear Winston Churchill's speech

587. A pair of African gaboon vipers, which were returned after one of them bit the boy (who survived)

588. The seated bronze statue is in a park at 11th Street & Massachusetts Avenue, N.W.

589. Blacks were assigned a roped-off section, separated by a dirt road

590. 1950

591. Who requested the Army Signal Corps to install stereo speakers under his bed, because that's where he liked to hear music coming from?

592. Which philanthropist gave the nation a treasured art collection with the stipulation that the gallery should not be named after him?

593. Who dreamed only a week before his assassination that he had been murdered?

594. Which celebrity operated the world's first public telegraph office when it opened in Washington in 1845?

595. What is the total length of corridors in the Department of Commerce building?

596. This First Lady planted the first roses in what became known as the White House Rose Garden

597. When did the first train arrive in the nation's capital?

598. In early 20th century Washington they were called Hurdy-Gurdy men. What were they?

ANSWERS

591. John Kennedy

592. Andrew Mellon

593. Abraham Lincoln

594. Samuel Morse

595. 8 miles

596. Ellen Wilson

597. 1835

598. Organ-grinders with monkeys

599. How long did it take Smithsonian experts to create the figures for the Neanderthal burial scene in the Museum of Natural History?

600. When did Congress wipe out the name Georgetown from the map of Washington?

601. What reason did Richard Nixon give for naming his Irish setter dog *King Timahoe*?

602. Where are the seals of the contiguous 48 states seen in stained glass windows?

603. Which former President became Chief Justice of the Supreme Court?

604. What is known as the Chief Guest House of the Nation?

605. Which 20th century leader said: "I have worked hard all my life. That's the only recipe for success I know"

606. Where can you get more than $100 for less than a dollar?

607. By what derisive name was early Washington known?

608. Why did the Ritz-Carlton concierge hastily pursue a hotel guest to New York?

ANSWERS

599. Over 3,000 man hours

600. 1895

601. He said it was the name of the village in Ireland where his mother's Quaker ancestors came from

602. Above the reading room in the Library of Congress

603. William Howard Taft

604. Blair House

605. Harry Truman

606. At the Bureau of Engraving & Printing, where defective bills are shredded and packaged for sale

607. "The mud-hole city"

608. To deliver a mink coat left behind

609. What was the name of the Presidential yacht used by McKinley, Teddy Roosevelt, Taft, Wilson, Coolidge and Harding?

610. Franklin Roosevelt and Winston Churchill prayed in adjoining pews in this church at the national Christmas service in 1941

611. Why did a 19-year-old Ohio woman shoot to death a clerk in the Treasury building?

612. What were *Queen Mary* and *Queen Elizabeth* doing in Washington during the Nixon administration?

613. Which painting in the National Gallery of Art was originally owned by King Henry VII of England, and later by Catherine the Great of Russia?

614. Who was the shortest President since the founding of the Republic?

615. Which graduate of Washington's Dunbar High School became the first black to command a U.S. Army division?

616. Where is the statue of 19th century Ukrainian nationalist and poet, Taras Shevchenko?

ANSWERS

609. The *Mayflower*

610. Foundry Methodist Church at 16th & Church Streets N.W.

611. She charged him with breach of promise to marry her

612. They were Secret Service black convertibles used for the White House

613. Raphael's *St. George and the Dragon*

614. James Madison, at 5'4"

615. Major General Frederic E. Davison

616. At the junction of 22nd & P Streets N.W.

617. Who phoned Sugar Ray Leonard the night before he became world champ, with advice not to do anything cute or flashy?

618. Which diplomatic wife was renowned for her sculptural talent?

619. In what mansion did Calvin Coolidge live while the White House was being renovated?

620. Which assassinated President gasped: "My wife—be careful about her. She's sleeping—break the news gently to her..."

621. Where did the original ticket booth from Yankee Stadium land up eventually?

622. Where is the monument to the Grand Army of the Republic?

623. How many pre-19th century books are in the U.S. Naval Observatory library?

624. This late Justice of the Supreme Court missed half a year of court work after being tossed from a horse, sustaining a punctured lung and broken ribs. Who was he?

625. Of what disease did Dolley Madison's first husband die?

ANSWERS

617. Muhammed Ali

618. Maria Martins, wife of the Brazilian Ambassador

619. The Patterson House at 15 Dupont Circle

620. William McKinley

621. In the baseball display section of the National Museum of American History

622. At the intersection of Indiana Avenue & 7th Streets N.W.

623. 800

624. William O. Douglas

625. Smallpox

QUESTIONS

626. She studied history of art at the Sorbonne in Paris, then American history at George Washington University, before her marriage to a man who became President

627. When did American University's faculty vote to admit black students?

628. Why did the demented Charles Guiteau kill President Garfield?

629. During whose administration were White House invitations first mailed instead of being delivered by messenger?

630. Who wrote of Washington: "The rents are high, the food is bad, the dust is disgusting, the mud is deep, and the morals are deplorable"?

631. Name the young English widower who emigrated to America and became famous as a capital architect

632. What is the most enduring legend of Octagon House?

633. Which country donated the 18 crystal chandeliers in the Kennedy Center's grand foyer?

ANSWERS

626. Jacqueline Kennedy

627. 1937

628. He felt rebuffed in seeking Government employment

629. Franklin Roosevelt's

630. Horace Greeley, owner of the New York *Herald*

631. Benjamin Latrobe

632. The ghost of an owner's daughter wanders about ever since she leapt from the staircase after a thwarted love affair

633. Sweden

634. Why did six Native American chiefs ride in Theodore Roosevelt's second inaugural parade?

635. What happened when arches collapsed under the Senate chamber in the Capitol in 1808?

636. What was Richard Nixon's favorite wine?

637. What percentage of the Washington area's hotel business do you think derives from business meetings, conventions and small company gatherings?

638. Who built the first private house on Lafayette Square?

639. What were the nicknames of the parents of former White House correspondent Dan Rather?

640. How did a Soviet budget for a Five-Year-Plan get linked to paintings that wound up in the National Gallery of Art in Washington?

641. When more than 600 acres of land were reclaimed from the Potomac flats, which parks were created?

ANSWERS

634. Roosevelt said he wanted "a picturesque touch of color," later adding, "I wanted to give the people a good show"

635. They killed the Clerk of Works, John Lenthal

636. 1966 Chateau Margaux

637. About 51 percent

638. Commodore Stephen Decatur, in 1819

639. His father was (Daniel) *Rags* and his mother (Berl) *Mutt*

640. They sold paintings for $7 million to raise money for their Plan and the buyer, Andrew Mellon, later gave them to the gallery

641. East and West Potomac Parks

642. Which former President died in the Capitol after mumbling: "This is the last of earth, but I am content"?

643. What was Herbert Hoover holding as he watched his White House office burn?

644. How many stamps make up the Smithsonian's National Philatelic Collection?

645. Why did the Secret Service check out a bitch named Pushinka who lived in the White House?

646. Which bridge did Air Florida Flight 90 crash into in January 1982?

647. Why was the finished statue of George Washington never placed in the Capitol Rotunda as planned?

648. When the Reagans invited Prince Charles to dinner they presented this specially prepared dessert. Describe it

649. Which party did the distinguished black, Major General Robert Elliott, represent as a Congressman from South Carolina 1871–74?

650. What gift died the same year it was given to President Reagan?

ANSWERS

642. John Quincy Adams

643. A lighted cigar

644. More than 14 million

645. The daughter of Soviet space dog, *Strelka*, she was a gift from Nikita Krushchev to President Kennedy and had to be cleared for electronic implants

646. The northbound span of 14th Street bridge

647. There were howls of dismay over the partially-clothed body

648. A crown topped with three feathers—part of his coat of arms—all shaped from ice cream

649. Republican

650. An elephant presented by the President of Sri Lanka

651. Who was *Star* Mary?

652. Why did Harry Truman host a dinner for Queen Juliana and Prince Bernhard of the Netherlands in the Carlton Hotel rather than in the White House?

653. Which First Family stabled a cow on White House grounds for fresh milk supplies?

654. When was the first bridge built across the Potomac River?

655. Who was the first Pope to visit Washington D.C.?

656. Who sculptured the heads of Albert Einstein in the grounds of the National Academy of Sciences, and John Kennedy in the Kennedy Center?

657. Which American woman was so honored by Congress that it voted her a seat on the Senate floor whenever she was present?

658. To which building did an architect refer when he said: "Only an inaugural ball or a thunderstorm could possibly fill the immense void"?

ANSWERS

651. The lady in tattered clothes who sold newspapers for much of the 19th century under the lamp post at 15th & F. Streets N.W.

652. The kitchen was not yet complete in the renovated White House

653. William Howard and Helen Taft

654. 1797

655. John Paul II

656. Robert Berks

657. Dolley Madison

658. The old Patent Office building at G & 8th Streets N.W.

659. Which statue was English novelist William Thackeray ridiculing when he said: "The hero is sitting in an impossible attitude, on an impossible horse, with an impossible tail"

660. Who took the Carters to dinner at the posh French restaurant, Le Lion d'Or, after Reagan won the election?

661. Who was undoubtedly the most colorful, if not controversial Congressman ever elected?

662. Which famous grandson of Alexander Graham Bell donated the inventor's manuscripts to the Library of Congress?

663. Who lives in the Georgetown mansion once owned by Abraham Lincoln's son, Robert?

664. Why did a local brewing company dump 60,000 gallons of cider into the Potomac in 1933?

665. Where did Beijing's diplomats live while their U.S. embassy was readied?

666. Where were the original sheets of the Declaration of Independence and the U.S. Constitution kept before removal to the National Archives?

ANSWERS

659. Andrew Jackson upon his "rocking horse" in Lafayette Square

660. Rosalynn's hairdresser

661. Major General Daniel Sickles (D-N.Y.) who served in the House 1857–61 and 1893–95. He was acquitted after shooting to death his wife's lover. He lost a leg at the battle of Gettysburg and donated it to the Armed Forces Museum. As Ambassador to Spain he allegedly had an affair with the Queen, then married her lady-in-waiting

662. Melville Bell Grosvenor, Chairman of the Board of the National Geographic Society

663. Ben Bradley, *Washington Post* executive editor, and his wife, Sally

664. It needed the storage space to age beer

665. The Mayflower Hotel

666. In the Library of Congress

667. In whose honor was the first inaugural ball held in Washington?

668. What was the name of the Presidential yacht upon which Richard Nixon cruised the Potomac so often?

669. What was the size of the hailstones which fell downtown on April 29, 1938?

670. Name the First Lady who enjoyed smoking a corn-cob pipe

671. He was one of the richest men in America while living in the building now housing the National Trust for Historic Preservation

672. How many lift locks are there between Georgetown and Cumberland, Md., the 184.5 mile length of the Chesapeake & Ohio Canal?

673. Why did Evalyn Walsh McLean wear the fabulous Hope Diamond and other jewelry during regular visits to World War II amputees at Walter Reed Hospital?

674. Which Watergate felon was robbed of the diamond engagement ring he gave his wife?

ANSWERS

667. James Madison

668. *Sequoia*

669. They had diameters the size of quarters

670. Margaret Taylor

671. Andrew Mellon

672. 74

673. She claimed they enjoyed looking at the jewelry

674. Jeb Stuart Magruder (as his wife prepared to relocate with all their possessions from Los Angeles)

QUESTIONS

675. "Wednesday Evenings" was the shorthand description for gatherings of learned scientists at the home of which great inventor?

676. Why did Dwight Eisenhower christen each of his Presidential planes *Columbine*?

677. The son of which self-made millionaire restaurateur and property owner became a Congressional page?

678. What act of nature saved Washington's buildings from further destruction by British soldiers in August 1814?

679. How did Grover Cleveland become the first chief executive to be interviewed by telephone?

680. Who earned the nickname *Chairman Skinflint* for being tight-fisted with disbursements and arrogant as Chairman of the House Administration Committee?

681. How many first class seats were reserved on a plane to bring Leonardo da Vinci's painting *Ginevra de' Benci* from Europe to the National Gallery of Art in Washington?

682. How large is Rock Creek Park?

ANSWERS

675. Alexander Graham Bell

676. It was the name of the official flower of Mamie Eisenhower's home state, Colorado

677. Ulysses Augur Sr.

678. A violent thunderstorm

679. By chance, he picked up the phone when a plucky journalist called the White House in the early days of telephones

680. Wayne Hays (D-Ohio)

681. Three; one for the painting and two for those escorting it

682. 1800 acres

683. From what point in Washington can distances to other parts of the nation be measured?

684. When this celebrated Swedish opera singer stayed at Willard's Hotel she was honored with visits by President Fillmore, Daniel Webster and many other fans

685. Why was Swiss-born White House chef, Henri Haller, so ecstatic soon after the Nixons moved in?

686. Frances Hodgson Burnett earned so much money by writing this novel that she built a fine home at 1770 Massachusetts Avenue N.W. and lived there for the rest of her life. Name the book

687. What was *Hoover's Lake*?

688. If you heard the term "the Other Body", what would it signify in Washington?

689. By what name is the giant cataract on the Potomac River known—where it plunges about 40 ft. over a series of ledges?

690. Where did Senator Barry Goldwater (R.-Ariz.) and his wife, Peggy, celebrate their 40th wedding anniversary?

ANSWERS

683. Zero Milestone—a block of granite in the Ellipse

684. Jenny Lind

685. It was the first time he could recall that a President went into the kitchen to congratulate him personally on the meal

686. *Little Lord Fauntleroy*

687. The result of torrential rainwater filling the excavations for the gigantic Department of Commerce building

688. Someone in the House of Representatives referring to the Senate, and vice-versa

689. Great Falls

690. Aboard the Presidential yacht *Sequoia*

691. If the drawbridge was raised on Memorial Bridge, how high would each "leaf" be?

692. Name the first black appointed to a Presidential staff in an executive capacity

693. Which chief executive did not see a map of the United States until he was 19?

694. What company is the largest private employer in the Washington area?

695. Who delayed her flight from the White House, as British troops approached, until a portrait of George Washington was cut from its frame and taken to safety?

696. Guess the nationality of the diplomat who moaned: "Washington, with its venison, wild turkeys, canvas backs, oysters, terrapins etc., furnished better viands than Paris—and only wanted cooks"

697. A watercolor of a horse and cart, painted by which former President, hung in Ronald Reagan's hospital suite while he recovered from gunshot wounds?

698. At which church did Harry Truman worship regularly?

ANSWERS

691. 92 ft. — equivalent to an 8-story building

692. E. Frederic Morrow, who, in 1955, was appointed administrative officer for special projects

693. Millard Fillmore

694. The Marriott Corporation

695. Dolley Madison

696. The Imperial Russian Minister to Washington, Baron Tuyl

697. Ulysses S. Grant

698. First Baptist Church at 16th & O Streets N.W.

699. What have the following in common: Geronimo, American Horse, Hollow Horn Bear, Quanah Parker, Little Plume, and Buckskin Charley?

700. How many works of art have been lost to fires in the Capitol?

701. How many times did the Washington *Senators* win the American League pennant?

702. Which embassy is located in the home once occupied by Herbert Hoover?

703. Who was the first black female cabinet member?

704. Name the Washingtonian who was the wife of the last Imperial Russian envoy to the USA

705. What scandal prompted Dwight Eisenhower to invite Ghana's Finance Minister to breakfast at the White House?

706. Name the plush residential complex that was home, at differing times, to Protocol Chief Emil Mosbacher, Federal Reserve Board Chairman Arthur Burns, Presidential speechwriter Pat Buchanan, and *Redskins* owner Jack Kent Cooke

ANSWERS

699. Native American Chiefs, they rode down Pennsylvania Avenue during Theodore Roosevelt's inaugural parade

700. 16 busts, 1200 medals, 20 portraits and 3 statues

701. Three

702. The Embassy of Burma

703. Patricia Harris—to the Department of Housing & Urban Development, 1977

704. Mary Beale

705. A Delaware restaurant had ejected the Ghanian because he was black

706. The Watergate

707. Which 19th century President was a strict teetotaler?

708. What is the explanation for the wife of Senator William Fulbright sharing her mink stole with him at a White House function?

709. What event brought about the first presidential inaugural medal?

710. Where can you view exhibits from the Philadelphia Centennial in 1876?

711. Which President said: "The unnecessary felling of a tree seems to me a crime little short of murder"?

712. Who was the daughter of a President and the wife of a Speaker of the House of Representatives?

713. Who remains the only First Lady born outside the United States?

714. From which States did the first blacks come to serve in
    a. The House of Representatives
    b. The Senate

715. What did John Wilkes Booth shout out immediately after shooting Abraham Lincoln?

ANSWERS

707. Rutherford Hayes

708. It was chilly outside as they watched a military panorama

709. Thomas Jefferson's swearing-in, 1801

710. In the Smithsonian's Arts & Industries Building

711. Thomas Jefferson

712. Alice Roosevelt Longworth

713. Louisa Catherine Johnson Adams (1775–1852) was born in London, England, to a British mother and an American father

714. a. South Carolina
     b. Mississippi

715. Sic Semper Tyrannis! (Always Thus to Tyrants)

716. At what time of the day did Secretary of State Henry Kissinger receive Nixon's written resignation from the Presidency?

717. By what name did Caroline Kennedy call her pet pony while she lived in the White House?

718. What used to be housed in the Executive Office Building?

719. Name the building to which architect Benjamin Latrobe referred when he said: "I have just completed a church that made many Washingtonians religious who had not been religious before"

720. Before he became an international figure, this man cabled his marriage proposal from London and she replied "Yes" from California. Who was he?

721. Which book lies by the bedside of former President Wilson in his home on S Street N.W.?

722. To which side is the eagle's head pointed in the nation's coat of arms?

723. Where is the location of the office desk of long-time FBI Director, J. Edgar Hoover?

ANSWERS

716. 11:35 a.m.

717. Macaroni

718. The Departments of State, Navy & War

719. St. John's Church, in Lafayette Square

720. Herbert Hoover

721. *Imitations of Christ,* by Thomas a Kempis

722. To the bird's right hand side

723. On public display at FBI headquarters

724. Why did nonagerian Washingtonian, Mary Henderson, leave her $6 million fortune to her Japanese secretary and nothing to her granddaughter?

725. What is the eternal link between Woodrow Wilson and Admiral Dewey?

726. Name the 121-acre man-made island near the western end of Memorial Bridge

727. Of all the plants at the U.S. Botanic Garden on Capitol Hill, which are considered the most sensational?

728. Name the title of the book co-authored by Dan Rather, when chief White House correspondent for CBS, and Gary Paul Gates

729. Guess the monthly salary of Washington's first police chief

730. How much money did an employee walk away with from the Bureau of Engraving & Printing before the Secret Service nabbed him?

731. Who lay in state in the Capitol Rotunda more than 8 decades after his death?

ANSWERS

724. She had disinherited her adopted grand-daughter after the latter tried to have her committed to a mental institution. But both the secretary and granddaughter made an out of court settlement after much wrangling

725. They are both buried in Washington Cathedral

726. Lady Bird Johnson Park, formerly known as Columbia Island

727. The orchid collection, from which several hundred bloom weekly

728. *The Palace Guard*

729. $16.66

730. $160,000 in $20 bills (in December 1953)

731. Pierre Charles L'Enfant, original planner of Washington D.C., whose remains were reinterred in Arlington National Cemetery in 1909

732. What was the nickname given Carl Bernstein while a reporter on the New Jersey *Journal*, before he helped expose the Watergate scandal?

733. Which President immediately dismissed his guests after one of them, a Haitian who was Dean of the Diplomatic Corps, died?

734. What were the two favorite indoor recreations of George Washington?

735. Name the Smithsonian Institution celebrity who wrote of the importance to him of smells, and of his mental association of horse manure with Florence, Italy

736. In 1960 Soviet Premier Nikita Khrushchev gave the people of the USA a Siberian Larch tree. Where is it growing?

737. Who said: "What Washington needs more than anything else is a good cleaning out"?

738. How long are the nature trails on Theodore Roosevelt Island?

739. Which President fathered the most children?

740. Where did John Kennedy worship in Georgetown?

ANSWERS

732. The Rotten Kid

733. Chester Arthur

734. Billiards and listening to the harp

735. Recently-retired Secretary, Dillon Ripley

736. At the National Arboretum

737. General Eisenhower, before his election to the Presidency

738. 2.5 miles

739. John Tyler sired 8 sons and 7 daughters by two wives

740. Holy Trinity Roman Catholic Church

741. What tune did the U.S. Marine Band strike up as President Ford led Queen Elizabeth of England to the dance floor?

742. Why was the 4¢ *Project Mercury* stamp produced in strictest secrecy by the Bureau of Engraving & Printing in 1962?

743. What was Lady Bird Johnson carrying when she moved into the White House after the Kennedy assassination?

744. How much did Florida real estate mogul Thomas Malloy pay at an auction sale for the Presidential yacht *Sequoia*?

745. Which future President placed an advertisement in the newspapers offering a $500 prize for the best plan for the new capital city?

746. What is The China Room?

747. How did pioneer female journalist Ann Royall finally get John Quincy Adams to answer her questions?

748. Where are the clothes worn by Abraham Lincoln the night he was killed?

ANSWERS

741. *The Lady Is A Tramp*

742. Because it was to be issued simultaneously with the completion of the first orbital flight by an American astronaut, and no one knew if the flight would succeed

743. A framed photograph of the late Speaker of the House, Sam Rayburn

744. $286,000

745. Thomas Jefferson

746. A White House Room displaying china used by past Presidents

747. She sat on his clothes while he was swimming in the Potomac

748. In the Lincoln Museum at Ford's Theatre